EMBROIDERED ANIMALS

Wild and Woolly Creatures to Stitch and Sew

YUMIKO HIGUCHI

T0351649

ROOST BOOKS

CONTENTS

INTRODUCTION

I chose animals as the theme for this book's collection of patterns. I started with beloved pets like dogs and cats, moving on to familiar farm animals and zoo inhabitants, animals frolicking in forests and grasslands, animals in quiet observation, animals dressed in cute costumes, and animals whose unique characteristics I was able to simplify and capture—gathering together a wide variety of animals to portray.

As my handiwork progressed, one stitch at a time, I was delighted by the richness of my encounters with these creatures—a charming expression or pose, the warmth conveyed in the signature patterns of their fur—and the range of personalities that emerged in the patterns.

Quite different from the lush freshness I experience when embroidering flowering plants, here I feel affection and delight.

Once I complete an embroidery pattern, I like to give a project a purpose. Putting it in a hoop or a frame and hanging it on the wall is nice, but I recommend making it into a craft project. These mascots can bring you luck, so having them with you all the time—while out shopping, while traveling, at school, at work, or on a first date—might increase the chance of good things happening. Children have their own strengths and weaknesses, but they can always feel reassured if they have their mascot with them. You have your family and your friends, and now you can also have these as your avatars.

I believe that embroidery has magical powers. Take special care with the thoughts and effort that you put into these small handmade creations.

Yumiko Higuchi

BEARS IN THE FOREST
Crossbody Bag

PAGE 80

I transformed a story featuring humorous forest animals into an oversized crossbody bag. The pattern is mature enough that even adults can use it, especially in these muted colors.

BIRDS IN PARADISE
Trifold Pouch

PAGE 81

This extravagant embroidery features images of graceful birds in their own paradise. Attach your choice of cord to this simple trifold pouch, and wind it around to safeguard your treasures.

BIRDS IN PARADISE

PAGE 60

DANGLING MONKEY

PAGE 62

Drawstring Backpack

PAGE 82

This knapsack is scattered with monkeys
hanging from vines, bananas, and palm trees.
The gray-and-yellow color combination suits
children and adults alike, regardless of gender.

Trivet Cushion

PAGE 83

Small flowers of the field and frolicking wild
rabbits are rendered in nostalgic hues. This
soft cushion will help keep a teapot warm—
so you can enjoy teatime with the bunnies!

WILD REINDEER

PAGE 64

Simple Bag

PAGE 84

These reindeer are ready for winter, with their full white coats grown in around their necks and their majestic antlers. Just their faces create an impressive presence! I embroidered them in a regular pattern on a simple, long, vertical bag.

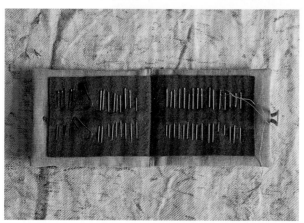

Needle Case

PAGE 84

This needle case has a neutral color scheme to complement embroidery hoops and other notions. Stuff it with quilt batting to keep your needles safe from damage.

Sachet

PAGE 85

This ornament features a beautiful pattern of a grazing giraffe, padded with soft and fluffy cotton. Tuck your choice of herbs inside and hang it in the closet.

Mini Tote Bag

PAGE 86

I surrounded the cheetah with flowers
and plants that grow in the jungle. The
bag may be small, but it has a big impact
as an accessory for your summer outfits.

Note Card

PAGE 86

Why not add a cute cat face to a tiny note card? Create an assortment by varying the colors or the pattern. Or change the cat's expression just by moving the position of the eyes or the way the mouth is set.

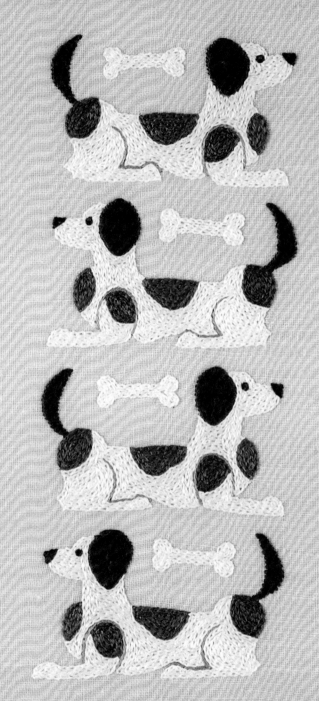

Tote Bag

PAGE 87

I imagined this tote bag as the perfect thing
to take on dog walks. You can scatter the
dog and bone motifs or create a repeating
pattern—it's adorable either way!

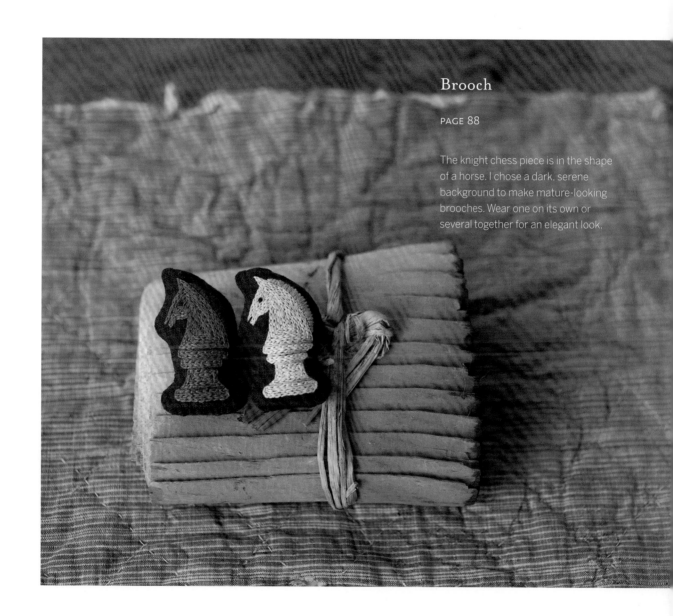

Brooch

PAGE 88

The knight chess piece is in the shape of a horse. I chose a dark, serene background to make mature-looking brooches. Wear one on its own or several together for an elegant look.

WOLVES AT NIGHT

PAGE 69

30

Drawstring Bag

PAGE 88

This pattern features wolves racing through the forest at nighttime. I chose a sweet rounded shape for this pochette. Just pull the string tight to close it and keep everything inside.

Charm Pouch

PAGE 89

For this little pouch, I embroidered an owl on the front and a moon on the back. You can sew this simple, unlined pouch by hand and offer your finished works as token gifts.

Triangular Flags

PAGE 90

This pattern features an adorable
elephant balancing on a ball. The tinkling
of the bells attached to the triangular
flags adds a joyful sound to a fun
decoration. Make as many as you like!

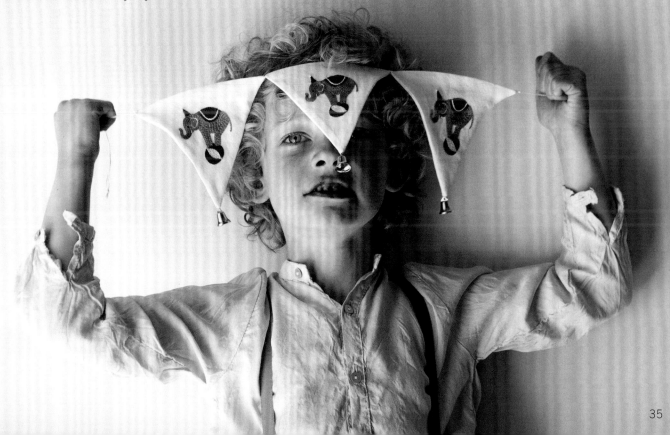

Scissors Case

PAGE 90

With two deer facing each other over a lovely rose, this emblem imparts a classic feel. The quilt padding inside keeps my beloved scissors safe and sound.

Bookmark

PAGE 91

Look to see how one of these cute stuffed teddy bears—with its round belly and padded paws—transforms into a panda! I recommend this simple bookmark as a project for those who are less confident with sewing.

ZEBRAS AND CACTI

PAGE 74

KOALA AND EUCALYPTUS LEAVES

PAGE 71

This cute koala, with his bushy ears, is climbing up the tree. This lion, king of the savanna, waits alone at night. Use an embroidery hoop as a frame to make an attractive decoration with either or both of these.

LONELY LION

PAGE 75

CAMEL WITH CARPETED SADDLE

PAGE 79

Embroidery Basics, Patterns, and Project Instructions

This section will introduce you to the art of embroidery and the basic stitches and skills you need to create beautifully finished embroidery work. All the patterns and instructions on how to make the projects are included.

TOOLS

1. CHALK PAPER Also called "transfer paper," this paper is used to transfer patterns onto fabric. For dark fabric, use white chalk paper.

2. TRACING PAPER This thin paper is another option for copying patterns.

3. CELLOPHANE Use this material to cover the tracing paper so it doesn't tear when you transfer patterns onto fabric.

4. TRACER Use this tool to trace the pattern when transferring onto fabric. You can also use a ballpoint pen.

5. EMBROIDERY HOOPS Use embroidery hoops to stretch fabric tightly. The hoop size will depend on the pattern size, but I recommend a 4" hoop.

6. NEEDLE THREADER This tool makes it easier to put the thread into the eye of a needle.

7. BODKIN Use this to thread [elastic or] the drawstring on a pouch.

8. NEEDLES AND PINCUSHION I use French embroidery needles with sharp points. The needle size depends on how many strands of No. 25 embroidery floss are used.

9. EMBROIDERY SCISSORS Small, sharp, pointed scissors with a thin edge are the easiest to use.

10. EYELETEER Use this tool for perforations.

11. TAILOR'S SHEARS It's best to have sharp shears that are specifically made for cutting fabric.

MATERIALS

No. 25 embroidery floss is the most popular. In this book, I used DMC embroidery floss from France, which is known for its vivid colors and lustrous texture.

All of the projects, including bags, are made using linen. Plain weave linen is easy to work with, can be washed, and has a smooth texture, so it's perfectly suited for embroidery fabric. It's best to wash linen before cutting it to size, then dry it away from direct sunlight. To readjust the fabric grain, iron the linen lightly before it's completely dry.

Choose the size of your needle based on the number of strands you are using. This way, you'll always have the perfect needle for whatever project you're working on. The thickness of the fabric you're using also determines the size. The standard sizes of Clover needles follow:

No. 25 Embroidery Floss	Embroidery Needle
6 strands	No. 3/4
3–4 strands	No. 5/6
1–2 strands	No. 7–10

Basic Stitches and Embroidery Fundamentals

Here are nine basic embroidery stitches. I'll also show you tricks for finishing your work beautifully.

STRAIGHT STITCH

This stitch is ideal for creating short lines. I use it to make whiskers or fur.

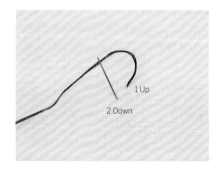

SECURELY FASTEN YOUR EMBROIDERY HOOP If your embroidery hoop is fastened too loosely, the fabric can sag and wrinkle. Take the time to wrap the inner hoop with bias tape or fabric (I recommend using white) to help prevent slippage. Once you've finishing wrapping the inner hoop, secure the end with a few stitches. When working with a larger pattern, you may need to slide the hoop over your work. To prevent delicate work from being damaged, place a patch of fabric over the embroidered section then fit the hoop.

OUTLINE STITCH

Use this for borders, as well as for stems and branches. This stitch creates a beautiful finish when sewing on an intricate curve.

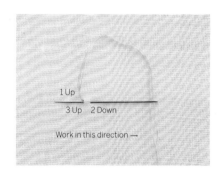

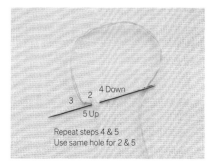

RUNNING STITCH

This stitch creates a quick and simple dotted line. Once you get the knack for this stitch, you can really run with it.

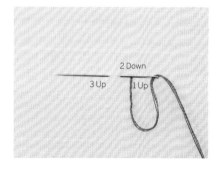

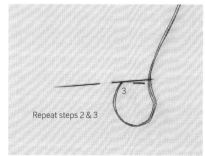

CHAIN STITCH

Use this stitch for lines or for filling in areas. To create a plump and pretty chain stitch, don't pull the thread too tight and keep the size of the loops uniform.

TIP End your chain of stitches with a lazy daisy stitch.

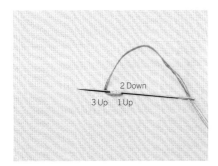

2 Down
3 Up   1 Up

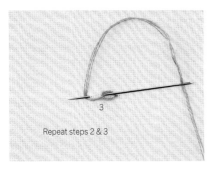

3

Repeat steps 2 & 3

LAZY DAISY STITCH

This stitch creates a small flower petal or a leaf. Maintain a full shape by gently pulling the thread into position.

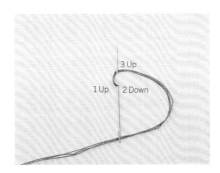

3 Up
1 Up   2 Down

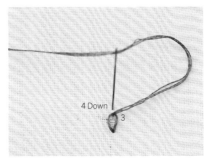

4 Down   3

LAZY DAISY STITCH + STRAIGHT STITCH

Sew one or two straight stitches across the center of the lazy daisy. It creates a full oval shape.

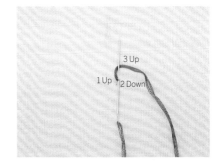

3 Up
1 Up   2 Down

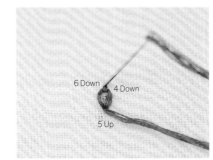

6 Down   4 Down
5 Up

FRENCH KNOT STITCH

The basic French knot stitch is a double wrap. Adjust the size based on the number of strands of thread. The knots are easily crushed, so work them as you finish a project.

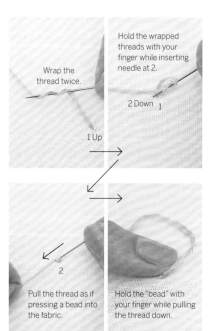

Wrap the thread twice.

Hold the wrapped threads with your finger while inserting needle at 2.

2 Down 1

1 Up

2

Pull the thread as if pressing a bead into the fabric.

Hold the "bead" with your finger while pulling the thread down.

SATIN STITCH

Work these stitches side by side to fill in an area. Line up the parallel threads and make sure they aren't twisted to create a beautiful finish.

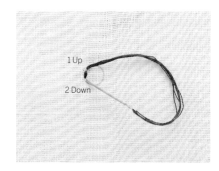

1 Up

2 Down

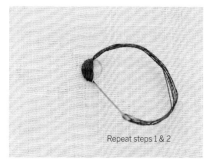

Repeat steps 1 & 2

FLY STITCH

This stitch creates a V or Y shape. Use it for the animal's nose or mouth.

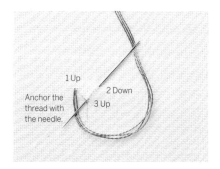

1 Up

2 Down

3 Up

Anchor the thread with the needle.

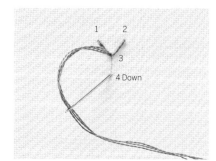

1   2

3

4 Down

TIPS FOR CHAIN STITCHES

FILLING IN AN AREA NEATLY (1) Be careful not to leave any gaps.

1

Sew the outline of the pattern.

2

Following the outline, sew the additional rows, working from the outside toward the inside. If a gap appears, go back at the end and fill in with more chain stitches or outline stitches.

TIPS FOR CHAIN STITCHES

FILLING IN AN AREA NEATLY (2) How to embroider an area that also has an inner border:

1

Sew both the outer and inner outlines of the pattern.

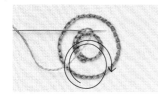

2

Following the inner outline, sew the additional rows, working from the inside toward the outside.

TIPS FOR CHAIN STITCHES

EMBROIDER NEAT ANGLES To create neat right angles when working chain stitches, the trick is to sew a bit to the inside, as shown, when you turn the angle.

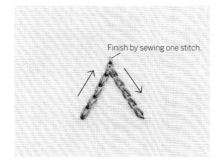

Finish by sewing one stitch.

TIPS FOR CHAIN STITCHES

EMBROIDER NEAT CIRCLES When creating a circle or an outline with chain stitches, make sure to connect the first and last stitches for a clean finish.

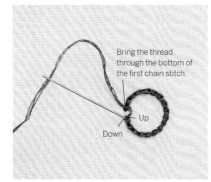

Bring the thread through the bottom of the first chain stitch.

Up

Down

TIPS FOR OUTLINE STITCHES

EMBROIDER GENTLE CURVES Bring the needle up, then down, then back up halfway between the previous stitch; repeat. To create an intricate curve, the trick is to make very fine stitches.

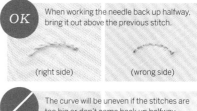

OK

When working the needle back up halfway, bring it out above the previous stitch.

(right side)   (wrong side)

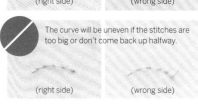

The curve will be uneven if the stitches are too big or don't come back up halfway.

(right side)   (wrong side)

EMBROIDERING WITH TWO COLORS OF THREAD AT A TIME

By using strands in two different colors, the color looks variegated and creates a deeper effect. I did this for the squirrels' tails and for the animals' fur.

1

Arrange the same lengths of the specified number of strands of each color of thread.

2

Pass the thread from step 1 through the needle. [Tie a knot at one end of the thread.] Embroider stitches as you normally would.

NEATENING YOUR FABRIC EDGE

Neatening your fabric edge will prevent the edges from fraying while you embroider and will make your work go more smoothly.

HIGH-COUNT (FINE) LINEN: Create a fringed edge on all four sides by gently unraveling the thread about ¼" on each side.

LOW-COUNT (COARSE) LINEN: Sew a rough whipstitch on all sides. Or use pinking shears to cut the fabric.

TRANSFERRING PATTERNS

First, locate the area where you will transfer the pattern to the fabric. Arrange the pattern along the warp and weft.

1 Place the tracing paper over the pattern, and transfer the design.

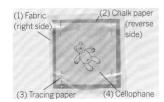

(1) Fabric (right side) (2) Chalk paper (reverse side)
(3) Tracing paper (4) Cellophane

2 Layer as shown in the photo, secure with pins, and trace the pattern using a tracer.

HOW TO HANDLE THREAD (1)

For No. 25 embroidery floss, pull a length of thread from the skein and separate the specified number of strands one at a time. Arrange them together with the ends aligned neatly.

1 Pull a standard length of 2' from the skein, and cut the thread.

2 One at a time, pull the number of strands you need, and arrange them together.

HOW TO HANDLE THREAD (2)

How you thread the desired number of strands through the needle differs depending on whether you're using an odd or even number of strands.

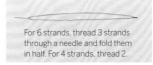

For 6 strands, thread 3 strands through a needle and fold them in half. For 4 strands, thread 2.

For even numbers of strands: For 2 strands, thread 1 length through the needle, fold it in half, align the ends, then make a knot.

For odd numbers of strands: Arrange the desired number of strands, thread the needle, and make a knot at one end.

KNOTS

Make a knot at the end of the thread when you start stitching embroidery for projects.

1 Thread the strands through the needle, place the end of the thread near the tip of the needle.

2 Wrap the thread twice around the tip of the needle.

3 Pinch the wrapped thread between your fingertips, slide it down the needle, and pull the knot all the way to the end of the thread.

WHEN SWITCHING THREAD

When you run out of thread or need to switch colors, start a new thread where stitches already exist.

(Reverse)

Weave a knotted length of thread around the stitches on the reverse, and bring the needle up at the starting point. Cut off the knot later.

STARTING YOUR EMBROIDERY (1)

Here's how to start embroidering when creating lines using chain or outline stitches.

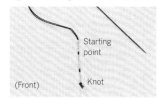

1 (Front)

Work a few small backstitches along a line toward the starting point, then bring the needle up at the starting point.

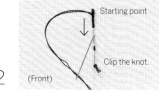

2 (Front)

Continue working, overlaying the stitches from step 1. When you reach the knot, clip it off.

STARTING YOUR EMBROIDERY (2)

Here's how to start embroidering when filling in areas using satin stitches.

1 (Front)

Work a few pick stitches (or short running stitches) along a line toward the starting point, then bring the needle up at the starting point.

2 (Front)

Continue working, covering the stitches from step 1, and when you reach the knot, clip it off.

FINISHING YOUR EMBROIDRY (1)

Here's how to finish embroidering once you've created lines using chain or outline stitches.

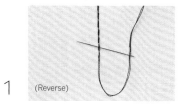

1 (Reverse)

Bring the needle up on the reverse side, and anchor the thread by wrapping it through several times around a stitch on this side.

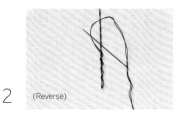

2 (Reverse)

Cut the end of the thread.

FINISHING YOUR EMBROIDERY (2)

Here's how to finish embroidering once you've filled in areas using satin stitches.

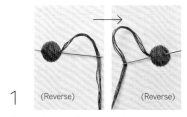

1 (Reverse)   (Reverse)

Bring the needle up on the reverse side, pass the thread under the stitches several times to anchor the thread.

2 (Reverse)

Cut the end of the thread.

MAKING NEAT SEAM ALLOW- ANCES FOR SMALL PROJECTS

Making cuts along the curves in the seam allowances for small projects will prevent the fabric from being too stiff when you turn it right side out. Be careful not to cut the backstitches. It's best to use pinking shears.

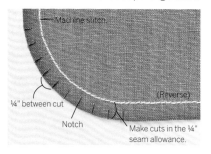

Machine stitch.

(Reverse)

¼" between cut

Notch

Make cuts in the ¼" seam allowance.

U-SHAPED LADDER STITCH

This stitch is used to close the opening for turning out because it creates an invisible seam.

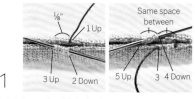

⅛"   Same space between

1 Up   5 Up   3 4 Down

1   3 Up   2 Down

Match up the folded edges, and pass the knotted thread to the front from the reverse side. Insert the needle into the edge facing it, and skim under the fabric edge.

2

Sew the edges together, creating a U-shape. Finish it off by tying a knot and hiding it on the reverse side.

*I used thread in a contrasting color to illustrate these steps. Use thread that matches the right side of your fabric.

BEARS IN THE FOREST

PAGE 8

For the animals, begin by working the edges of the eyes and mouth. Next, work the outline of the silhouette, and then fill in the rest. The trick is not to make the eyes too small—be sure to leave enough space around the opening.

Lazy daisy + straight (6) 3033

French knot (6) 3033

Outline 310

Work straight stitch for short lines 310

French knot (6) 3033

Outline 310

Work straight stitch for short lines 310

Straight 310

French knot (4) 3033

Work straight stitch for short lines 310

Outline 310

Outline 310

Straight (4) 3033

Align facing pattern pages along this line

58

- DMC No. 25 embroidery floss: 310, 3033
- For eyes and noses of animals, work French knots (4) 310.

- Work chain stitch (2 strands) 310, unless noted otherwise.
- Use 2 strands, unless noted otherwise.
- The number in parentheses is the number of strands, followed by the color code or name for the DMC No. 25 embroidery floss.

Align facing pattern pages along this line.

Running (4) 3033

Straight (6) 3033

Straight 310

French knot (4) 3033

Outline 310

Lazy daisy + straight (4) 3033

Outline 310

BIRDS IN PARADISE

PAGE 10

For the entire pattern, work the chain stitches first, followed by outline stitches. If you fill in the birds' eyes, work the French knots (4) in a different color.

Lazy daisy + straight (4)

French knot (6)

Lazy daisy + straight (6)

- DMC No. 25 embroidery floss: 712
- For birds' beaks, work straight stitch (2).
- For plants, work outline stitch (4) for thick lines, (2) for thin lines. Work French knots (6) for dots.
- Work chain stitch, unless noted otherwise.
- The number in parentheses is the number of strands, followed by the color code or name for the DMC No. 25 embroidery floss.

Straight (2)

French knot (6)

Align facing pattern pages along this line.

Lazy daisy + straight (4)

Lazy daisy + straight (6)

61

DANGLING MONKEY

PAGE 12

Begin by working the chain stitches first. For the monkey, work the face, next the stomach, then the ears, and finish by filling in the body with chain stitches. Add the eyes and nose last.

- DMC No. 25 embroidery floss: 645, 648, 842, 310, 733, 505, 739, 611
- Work chain stitch (2), unless noted otherwise.
- The number in parentheses is the number of strands, followed by the color code or name for the DMC No. 25 embroidery floss.

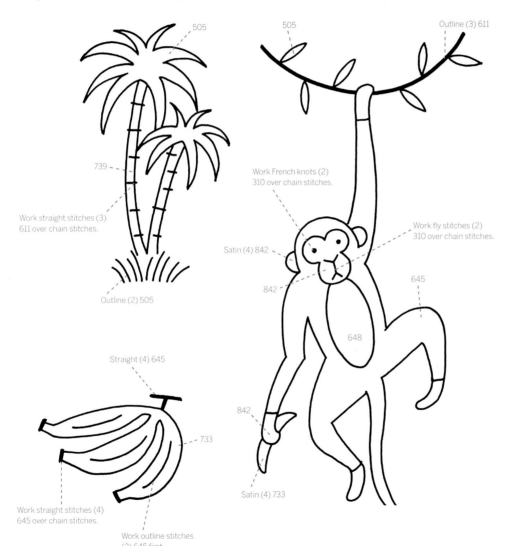

505

505

Outline (3) 611

739

Work French knots (2)
310 over chain stitches.

Work fly stitches (2)
310 over chain stitches.

Work straight stitches (3)
611 over chain stitches.

Satin (4) 842

842

842

645

648

Outline (2) 505

Straight (4) 645

842

733

Satin (4) 733

Work straight stitches (4)
645 over chain stitches.

Work outline stitches
(2) 645 first.

DANCING RABBITS

PAGE 14

For the rabbits, begin with the eyes. After working the French knots for the pupils, work a delicate round of outline stitches. Then fill in the body with chain stitches. Leave a gap where the legs overlap with the torso.

- DMC No. 25 embroidery floss: 3031, ecru, 739, 3051, 3777, 823, 830, 310
- Work outline stitch (2) for plant stems.
- Work chain stitch (2), unless noted otherwise.
- The number in parentheses is the number of strands, followed by the color code or name for the DMC No. 25 embroidery floss.

Work straight stitches (4) 310 over chain stitches.

Leave a gap where the legs overlap with the torso.

French knot (4) 823

Satin (4) 739

3031

French knot (4) 739

3051

French knot (6) 823

3051

French knot (4) 3031

3031

Straight (6) 3777

French knot (4) 310

Outline (2) ecru

3031

Lazy daisy + straight (6) 3031

Lazy daisy + straight (6) 3777

3031

Edge of trivet cushion pattern

3051

3051

French knot (4) 739

Lazy daisy + straight (4) 830

Lazy daisy + straight (6) 3051

WILD REINDEER

PAGE 16

For the antlers, work satin stitches out from the center.
Next, work the chain stitches for the face, followed by the
ears, eyes, nose, and mouth.
For their winter coats, work radially and fill in with thick
outline stitches.

- DMC No. 25 embroidery floss: 926, 08, ecru, 310
- Use 6 strands, unless noted otherwise.
- The number in parentheses is the number of strands,
  followed by the color code or name for the DMC No. 25
  embroidery floss.

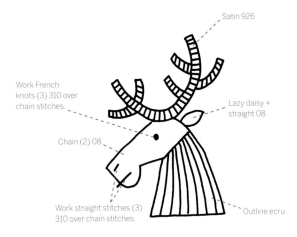

Satin 926

Work French
knots (3) 310 over
chain stitches.

Lazy daisy +
straight 08

Chain (2) 08

Work straight stitches (3)
310 over chain stitches.

Outline ecru

WOOLLY SHEEP

PAGE 18

Begin by working the chain stitches in black, then work
the ears, eyes, and nose evenly over the chain stitches.
Try to work the outline stitches delicately.

- DMC No. 25 embroidery floss: 310, 712, 3790
- Use 2 strands, unless noted otherwise.
- The number in parentheses is the number of strands,
  followed by the color code or name for the DMC No.
  25 embroidery floss.

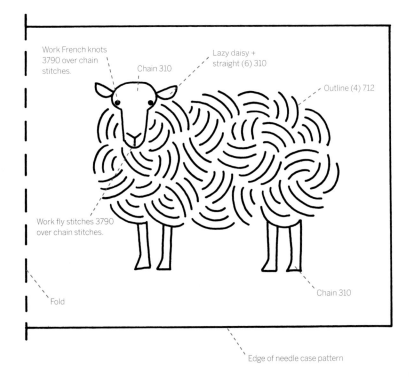

Work French knots
3790 over chain
stitches.

Chain 310

Lazy daisy +
straight (6) 310

Outline (4) 712

Work fly stitches 3790
over chain stitches.

Chain 310

Fold

Edge of needle case pattern

GIRAFFES ON THE SAVANNA

PAGE 20

The degree of difficulty for this pattern is slightly higher. Begin by working the chain stitches for the body, then fill in the pattern with satin stitches. Work the eyes, nose, hooves, and mane last.

After completing the giraffe, work the grass under its feet in chain stitches.

Work the trees, saving the leaves for last.

- DMC No. 25 embroidery floss: 712, 829, 938, 520, 522, 310, 610
- For the giraffe's eyes, work French knots (4), and for the eyelashes and nose, work straight stitches—all in 310 over chain stitches.
- Work chain stitch (2 strands), unless noted otherwise.
- Use 2 strands, unless noted otherwise.
- The number in parentheses is the number of strands, followed by the color code or name for the DMC No. 25 embroidery floss.

Satin (4) 938

Satin (4) 829

Outline 712

712

712

French knot (4) 829

Straight (4) 829

Straight (4) 938

712

520

Work satin stitches (4) 938 over chain stitches.

Work straight stitches 522 over chain stitches.

610

Lazy daisy + straight (4) 520

Outline (4) 938

520

Outline 543

Work over chain
stitches 890

Edge of mini tote
bag pattern

520

French knot
(4) 3046

3687

French knot
(6) 543

Work French knots
3371 over chain
stitches.

Outline (3) 869

890

Work satin stitches
3371 over chain
stitches.

833

3046

Work straight stitches
3371 randomly over
chain stitches.

Leave a gap where the
legs overlap the torso.

3046

Outline 890

890

520

520

Fold

CHEETAH IN THE JUNGLE

PAGE 22

For the cheetah, begin by working the chain stitches.
Leave a gap where the legs overlap with the torso.
For the pattern, work small straight stitches randomly
over the chain stitches. For the plants, begin by working
the chain stitches. Work the French knots last.

- DMC No. 25 embroidery floss: 833,
  3046, 3371, 869, 890, 520, 3687, 543
- For the thick lines of the plant stems,
  work outline stitch (4).
- Work chain stitch (2 strands), unless
  noted otherwise.
- Use 2 strands, unless noted
  otherwise.
- The number in
  parentheses is
  the number of strands,
  followed by the color
  code or name for the
  DMC No. 25
  embroidery floss.

733
Work straight stitches (4)
3021 over chain stitches.
08
310
310
Satin (6) ecru
3865

407
407
645
3865
794
Satin (6) ecru

Satin (6) 645
3812
310
648
648
648

645
733
Satin (6)
648
310
310

310
Satin (6) 738
310
310
3828
3812
Work straight stitches (4)
829 over chain stitches.

CAT FACES

PAGE 24

Start with the eyes. Work French knots for the
pupils and circle them with chain stitches.
Once you've worked the satin stitches for the
bridge of the nose and the jowls, you can move on
to the chain stitches for the rest of the head. Save
the nostrils, mouth, and whiskers for last.
Work thick straight stitches for the nostrils and a
delicate fly stitch for the mouth—all evenly over the
satin stitches

310
794
407
3021
3865
829
Satin (6) ecru

645
310
733
Satin (6) ecru
3865
407

- DMC No. 25 embroidery floss: 3865, ecru, 733, 407, 794, 648, 645, 3812, 08, 3021, 738, 3828, 829, 310
- For the cat eyes, work French knots (6) 310 for the pupils and chain stitches (3) for the irises.
- For the cat nostrils, work straight stitches (6); for the mouth, work fly stitch (3); and for the whiskers, work straight stitches (1).
- Work chain stitch (2 strands), unless noted otherwise.
- The number in parentheses is the number of strands, followed by the color code or name for the DMC No. 25 embroidery floss.

DOGS AND BONES

PAGE 26

Begin by working the satin stitches for the ears and the tail. Next, work the outline stitches for the thick lines where the legs overlap the torso. Then, fill in the areas with chain stitches. Leave the eye and nose for last.

- DMC No. 25 embroidery floss: 3865, 3799, 801, 829, 08, 07
- For the dog's eye, work French knots (4), and for the nose, work satin stitches (4)—both in 3799 over chain stitches.
- Work chain stitch (2 strands), unless noted otherwise.
- The number in parentheses is the number of strands, followed by the color code or name for the DMC No. 25 embroidery floss.

KNIGHT

PAGE 28

Work the parts with outline stitches before filling in the body with chain stitches.
Save the satin stitches of the mane for last.

- DMC No. 25 embroidery floss: 3031, 829, 310, 02, 03
- For the horse's eye, work French knots (2), and for the nose, work straight stitches (2)—both in 310 over chain stitches.
- Use 2 strands, unless noted otherwise.
- The number in parentheses is the number of strands, followed by the color code or name for the DMC No. 25 embroidery floss.

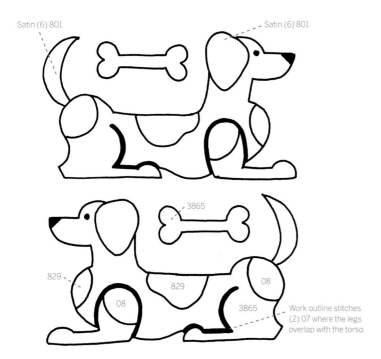

Satin (6) 801

Satin (6) 801

3865

829

08

829

08

3865

Work outline stitches (2) 07 where the legs overlap with the torso.

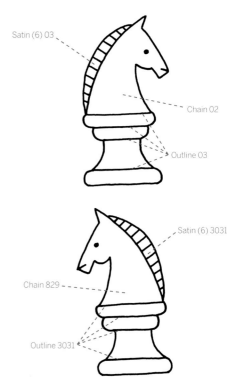

Satin (6) 03

Chain 02

Outline 03

Satin (6) 3031

Chain 829

Outline 3031

WOLVES AT NIGHT

PAGE 30

This pattern features lots of sharp angles worked in chain stitch.
Working these points as delicately as possible will give you a beautiful finish.
Save the three-dimensional stitches for last.

- DMC No. 25 embroidery floss: 3768, 733, 319, 3790
- Work chain stitch (2 strands), unless noted otherwise.
- Use 2 strands, unless noted otherwise.
- The number in parentheses is the number of strands, followed by the color code or name for the DMC No. 25 embroidery floss.

319

Outline (3) 3790

OWLS AND MOONS

PAGE 32

Do the eyes first. After working the French knots for the pupils, encircle them with delicate chain stitches. Next, work another circle of chain stitches, then continue by filling in the body. Work the branch next. Lastly, work the feathers, the beak, and the talons.

- DMC No. 25 embroidery floss: 3865, 834, 08, 07, 3371, 310
- Work chain stitch (2 strands), unless noted otherwise.
- Use 2 strands, unless noted otherwise.
- The number in parentheses is the number of strands, followed by the color code or name for the DMC No. 25 embroidery floss.

Work French knot 733 over chain stitches.

3768

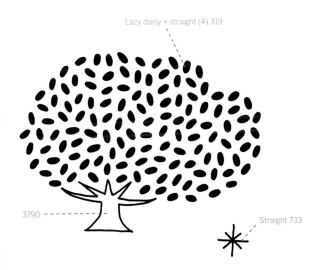

Lazy daisy + straight (4) 319

3790

Straight 733

07

3865

08

French knot (4) 310

Straight (4) 834

Work straight stitches (4) 07 over chain stitches.

Work straight stitches 3371 over chain stitches.

Outline 310

310

Straight (4) 834

834

CIRCUS ELEPHANTS

PAGE 34

First, work the outline stitches for the ears and the decoration on the costume on the elephant's back.
Next, move on to working the chain stitches.
Once you've worked the hat, the eye, and the mouth, you're all done.

• DMC No. 25 embroidery floss: 22, 712, 646, 310
• Work the French knots (2) 310 for the elephant's eye, and straight stitches (2) for the mouth; work these over the chain stitches.
• Work chain stitch (2 strands), unless noted otherwise.
• The number in parentheses is the number of strands, followed by the color code or name for the DMC No. 25 embroidery floss.

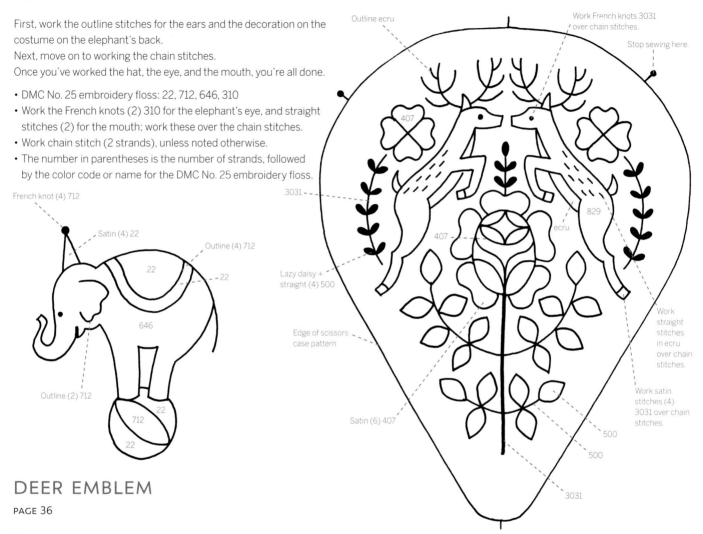

French knot (4) 712

Satin (4) 22

Outline (4) 712

22

22

646

Outline (2) 712

712

22

22

Outline ecru

Work French knots 3031 over chain stitches.

Stop sewing here.

407

3031

407

829

ecru

Lazy daisy + straight (4) 500

Edge of scissors case pattern

Satin (6) 407

500

500

3031

Work straight stitches in ecru over chain stitches.

Work satin stitches (4) 3031 over chain stitches.

DEER EMBLEM

PAGE 36

Begin with the chain stitches for the bodies of the deer. Work the chain stitches for the pattern on their backs and the satin stitches for the hooves over the chain stitches. For the rose, start with the outline stitches of the center stem. The many curves here require a delicate hand.

• DMC No. 25 embroidery floss: ecru, 829, 3031, 500, 407
• For the flower stems, work outline stitch (4) for thick lines and (2) for thin lines.
• Work chain stitch (2 strands), unless noted otherwise.
• Use 2 strands, unless noted otherwise.
• The number in parentheses is the number of strands, followed by the color code or name for the DMC No. 25 embroidery floss.

TEDDY BEARS AND PANDA

PAGE 38

First, work the chain stitches for the center of the face and the satin stitches for the paw.

Next, fill in the chain stitches for the rest of the body.

If gaps appear in your work, fill them in with chain or outline stitches.

For the panda, start by working the chain stitches for the eyes.

Do the ears after the chain stitches for the body. Leave the eyes, nose, claws, and navel for last.

- DMC No. 25 embroidery floss: 3866, 613, 08, 310
- For the bear's and panda's mouth and navel, and the claws on the bear's hind legs, work straight stitch (2) 310—all of these over the chain stitches.
- Work chain stitch (2 strands), unless noted otherwise.
- Use 2 strands, unless noted otherwise.
- The number in parentheses is the number of strands, followed by the color code or name for the DMC No. 25 embroidery floss.

KOALA AND EUCALYPTUS LEAVES

PAGE 43

Begin with the satin stitches for the nose. Next, work the chain stitches for the face and body.

For the ears, use two colors of thread (see p. 55). When the koala is finished, work the outline stitches for the tree, fill it in with chain stitch, and then work the leaves.

Don't forget to do the koala's claws at the end!

- DMC No. 25 embroidery floss: 3866, 01, 03, 08, 07, 844, 310, 501
- Work chain stitch (2 strands), unless noted otherwise.
- Use 2 strands, unless noted otherwise.
- The number in parentheses is the number of strands, followed by the color code or name for the DMC No. 25 embroidery floss.

Satin (6) 08

Work French knots 310 over chain stitches.

3866

Lazy daisy + straight (4) 310

08

French knot 310

Satin (6) 310

3866

613

Satin (6) 310

08

310

Work lazy daisy + straight stitches (4) 310.

3866

310

310

Outline 07

Lazy daisy + straight (4) 501

Work chain stitches 3866 in between outline stitches.

Work French knots (4) 310 over chain stitches.

Outline (4) 01 + 03 (combine 2 strands each)

Work straight stitches 310 over chain stitches.

Work straight stitches 310 over chain stitches.

01

03

Satin (6) 844

Outline 501

08

Outline 07

PIGLETS IN THE GARDEN

PAGE 40

It's best to start by working the green parts of the flowers. Work the three-dimensional aspects of the flowers last. For the piglets, start with the legs and tail, fill in the torso, and then move on to the ears, nose, and eyes—in that order.

Straight (6) 833

Straight (2) 505

505

Outline (2) 842

842

Work lazy daisy + straight stitches 407.

Work straight stitches (6) 407 over chain stitches.

Work French knots (2) 3787 over chain stitches.

French knot 739

932

505

French knot 3350

Satin (6) 3350

French knot 842

505

French knot 739

Outline (2) 407

Lazy daisy + straight (6) 407

505

French knot (6) 739

Lazy daisy + straight 505

Outline (2) 739

28   29   28

505

Lazy daisy + straight (2) 505

Align facing pattern pages along this line.

- DMC No. 25 embroidery floss: 505, 739, 833, 932, 3787, 28, 29, 407, 3350, 842
- For plant stems, work outline stitch (2) 505, unless noted otherwise.
- Work chain stitch (2 strands), unless noted otherwise.
- Use 2 strands, unless noted otherwise.
- The number in parentheses is the number of strands, followed by the color code or name for the DMC No. 25 embroidery floss.

Work outline stitches (2) 3787 over chain stitches.

505

Work French knots (2) 3787 over chain stitches.

833

Lazy daisy + straight 505

French knot 739

28

29

28

Work straight stitches (6) 739 over chain stitches.

505

French knot 3350

French knot 932

505

Lazy daisy + straight 505

505

739

French knot 833

ZEBRAS AND CACTI

PAGE 42

For the zebra's stripes, start by working the black chain stitches. Then, fill in the areas with the white chain stitches. When you've finished all the chain stitches, work the mane and tail.

- DMC No. 25 embroidery floss: 310, 3866, 319, 520
- Work chain stitch (3 strands), unless noted otherwise.
- Use 3 strands, unless noted otherwise.
- The number in parentheses is the number of strands, followed by the color code or name for the DMC No. 25 embroidery floss.

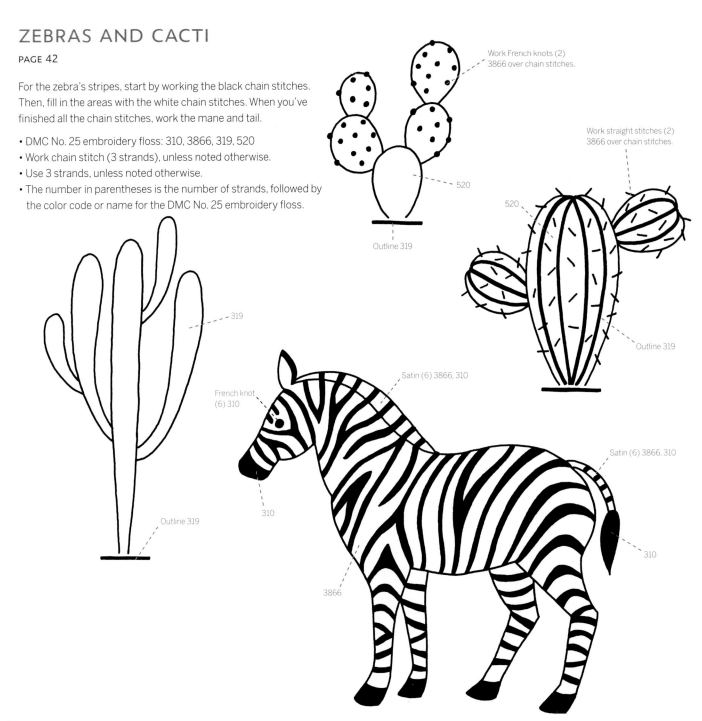

Work French knots (2) 3866 over chain stitches.

520

Outline 319

Work straight stitches (2) 3866 over chain stitches.

520

Outline 319

319

Outline 319

Satin (6) 3866, 310

French knot (6) 310

Satin (6) 3866, 310

310

310

3866

LONELY LION

PAGE 43

Begin with the eyes. Work the French knots for the pupils and circle them with chain stitches.

Next, work the satin stitches for the nose. Then move on to the chain stitches.

Fill in the mane, the torso, and the tail—in that order.

- DMC No. 25 embroidery floss: 3866, 739, 422, 839, 844, 890, 310
- Work chain stitch (2 strands), unless noted otherwise.
- Use 6 strands, unless noted otherwise.
- The number in parentheses is the number of strands, followed by the color code or name for the DMC No. 25 embroidery floss.

Lazy daisy + straight (4) 890

Straight 310

Satin 839

Work straight stitches (2) 839 over chain stitches.

French knot 310

422

3866

Satin 739

Satin 310

French knot (1) 844

3866

739

422

Straight (4) 890

839

422

Outline (2) 839

844

Straight (3) 310

Satin 839

Outline 422

Work straight stitches (2) 890 over chain stitches.

Work straight stitches (2) 310 over chain stitches.

SQUIRRELS AND ACORNS

PAGE 44

Start with the eyes. Work the French knots for the pupils and circle them with a delicate round of outline stitches.

For the tail, use two colors of thread (see p. 55). Work straight stitches randomly to create a sense of the direction of the fur.

- DMC No. 25 embroidery floss: 918, 3033, 310, 838, 3864, 3862, 3787, 640
- For the squirrels' eyes, work the pupils with French knots (4) 310 and delicately circle the eye with outline stitches (2) 3033. For the nose, work a fine straight stitch (4) 310.
- Work chain stitch (2 strands), unless noted otherwise.
- Use 2 strands, unless noted otherwise.
- The number in parentheses is the number of strands, followed by the color code or name for the DMC No. 25 embroidery floss.

3787

Work outline stitches 3862 over chain stitches.

Satin (4) 3864

838

3787

French knot (6) 3033

Follow the direction of the fur by randomly working straight stitches (4) 3033 + 918 (combine 2 strands each).

Satin (6) 838

918

Outline 640

Leave a gap where the leg overlaps with the torso.

Satin (6) 838

French knot (4) 3864

Outline 3862

FOX AND GRAPES

PAGE 45

First work the chain stitches.

For the fox, start with the face. Next, work the torso and the legs, in that order.

On the parts of the body that overlap, leave a gap of about 1 mm.

Leave the French knots for last because they are easily crushed.

- DMC No. 25 embroidery floss: 3865, 921, 310, 840, 520, 29
- For the fox's eyes, work French knots (4), and for the nose, work satin stitches (4)—both in 310 over chain stitches.
- Work chain stitch (2 strands), unless noted otherwise.
- Use 2 strands, unless noted otherwise.
- The number in parentheses is the number of strands, followed by the color code or name for the DMC No. 25 embroidery floss.

520

520

Outline 520

3865

3865

921

921

Straight (1) 310

Outline 520

French knot (6) 29

Leave a 1-mm gap where the body parts overlap.

310

840

Outline 840

COWS' WALTZ

PAGE 46

Begin by working the chain stitches for the face. Then work the satin stitches for the nose and hooves overlaying the chain stitches. Finish with the eyes and ears.

- DMC No. 25 embroidery floss: 310, 3866, 3864, 761
- Work chain stitch (2 strands), unless noted otherwise.
- Use 4 strands, unless noted otherwise.
- The number in parentheses is the number of strands, followed by the color code or name for the DMC No. 25 embroidery floss.

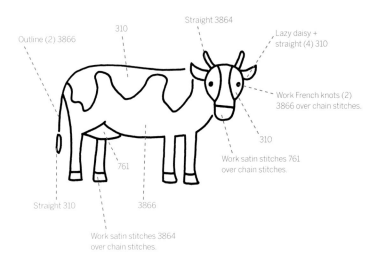

Outline (2) 3866

310

Straight 3864

Lazy daisy + straight (4) 310

Work French knots (2) 3866 over chain stitches.

310

Work satin stitches 761 over chain stitches.

761

Straight 310

3866

Work satin stitches 3864 over chain stitches.

RAFT OF DUCKS

PAGE 47

Begin by filling in with the chain stitches. Next, work the satin stitches for the beak. Finish with the eyes and nostrils.

- DMC No. 25 embroidery floss: 310, 3865, 648, 733, 08, 3768, 890
- Work chain stitch (2 strands), unless noted otherwise.
- Use 2 strands, unless noted otherwise.
- The number in parentheses is the number of strands, followed by the color code or name for the DMC No. 25 embroidery floss.

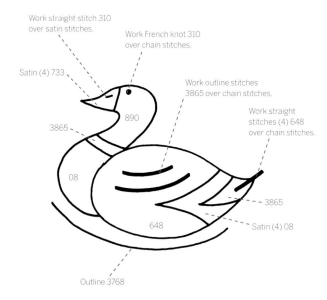

Work straight stitch 310 over satin stitches.

Work French knot 310 over chain stitches.

Satin (4) 733

Work outline stitches 3865 over chain stitches.

Work straight stitches (4) 648 over chain stitches.

3865

890

08

3865

648

Satin (4) 08

Outline 3768

CAMEL WITH CARPETED SADDLE

PAGE 48

The degree of difficulty for this pattern is slightly higher. Begin by working the satin stitches for the carpet. Make sure the threads don't get twisted. Work the straight stitches for the pattern, overlaying the satin stitches. After completing the carpet, work the satin stitches for the eyelid. Then fill in the body of the camel with chain stitches. Save the French knots for last.

- DMC No. 25 embroidery floss: 310, 3031, 3045, 3777, 3866, 3799
- For the camel's eye, nose, and mouth, work straight stitches (2) 310 over chain stitches.
- For the carpet's pattern, work French knots (4) for the circles and straight stitches (4) for the short lines.
- Work chain stitch (2 strands), unless noted otherwise.
- The number in parentheses is the number of strands, followed by the color code or name for the DMC No. 25 embroidery floss.

Satin (4) 3045

Work French knots (2) 310 over chain stitches.

3031

Satin (4) 3777

3866

3799

3799

3866

3866

3866

3799

3866

3799

3866

Outline (2) 3866

Work straight stitches (4) 3031 over chain stitches.

3045

310

Satin (4) 3045

Work French knots (6) 3866 over chain stitches.

Work straight stitches (2) 3777 over chain stitches.

Satin (4) 3866

79

BEARS IN THE FOREST
Crossbody Bag

PAGE 6

FINISHED SIZE
15¾" x 9" (main part of bag)

NO. 25 EMBROIDERY FLOSS
DMC 310, 3033, 3 skeins each

MATERIALS
Exterior fabric: Linen, moss green,
   17¾" x 11¾", 2 pieces
Lining fabric: Linen, white, 17¾" x 9¾",
   2 pieces
Facing fabric: Linen, moss green, 17¾" x 6"
Shoulder strap fabric: Linen, moss green,
   35½" x 4¾"
*If you want to reinforce the shoulder
   strap, apply fusible interfacing.
¼"-diameter snap fastener, antique gold,
   1 set
Machine-sewing thread, moss green, as
   needed

HOW TO MAKE

1 Using an iron, press folds into the fabric
for the shoulder strap as shown, and
machine stitch.

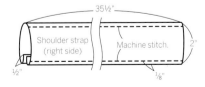

2 Transfer the embroidery pattern (p. 92) onto
the right side of the front exterior of the bag,
as shown. Embroider the pattern, and iron
your work lightly. Trace the pattern edges
onto the reverse side, and cut the fabric,
adding a ½" seam allowance all around. Cut
another exterior piece of fabric.

Front exterior (right side)
Work embroidery.
*2 pieces

3 For the facing fabric and the lining fabric,
trace the finished dimensions, as shown,
below on the reverse side of each piece.
Cut two pieces of each, adding a ½" seam
allowance on all four sides.

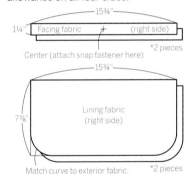

15¾"
1¼" Facing fabric (right side)
Center (attach snap fastener here)
*2 pieces

15¾"
7⅞"
Lining fabric (right side)
Match curve to exterior fabric.
*2 pieces

4 Assemble one piece of facing fabric and one
piece of lining fabric from step 3, right sides
together, and sew. Attach the snap fastener
to the right side of the facing fabric. Repeat
for the other pieces of facing and lining fabric.

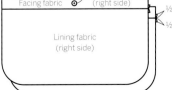

Attach snap at center (both pieces).
Facing fabric (right side)
½"
½"
Lining fabric (right side)

5 Assemble the exterior fabric from step 2.
With right sides together, sew along the
sides and bottom, leaving the mouth open.
Sew the facing and lining fabric from step
4 in the same way, leaving an opening for
turning out. Make cuts along the seam
allowances of the curves.

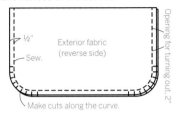

½"
Sew.
Exterior fabric (reverse side)
Opening for turning out, 2"
Make cuts along the curve.

6 Assemble the exterior bag and interior bag
from step 5 with right sides together. Insert
the shoulder strap fabric from step 1 at both
sides, between the exterior and interior
bags, with 1½" protruding. Sew all the way
around the mouth of the bag.

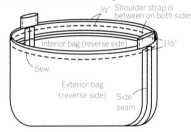

½" Shoulder strap is between on both sides.
Interior bag (reverse side)
1½"
Sew.
Exterior bag (reverse side)
Side seam

7 Turn the bag right side out, and lightly iron
to reshape. With a U-shaped ladder stitch,
sew the opening closed. Reinforce the side
seams where the base of the shoulder strap
attaches by machine stitching on the outside.

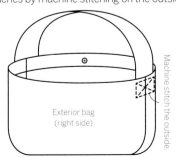

Exterior bag (right side)
Machine stitch the outside.

BIRDS IN PARADISE
Trifold Pouch

PAGE 7

FINISHED SIZE
5¼" x 7½"

NO. 25 EMBROIDERY FLOSS
DMC 3768, 6 skeins

MATERIALS
Exterior fabric: Linen, unbleached,
   17¾" x 10"
Lining fabric 1: Linen, unbleached, 6" x 10"
Lining fabric 2: Linen, white, 11¾" x 10"
⅛"-wide linen ribbon, unbleached, 25¾"
*It's a lovely touch to attach your choice
   of tassel to the ends of the ribbon.
Machine-sewing thread, unbleached, as
   needed

HOW TO MAKE

1 Transfer the embroidery pattern
(p. 60–61) onto the right side of the
exterior fabric, as shown. Embroider the
pattern, and iron your work lightly. Trace
the pattern edges onto the reverse side,
and cut the fabric, adding a ½" seam
allowance on all four sides.

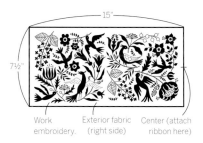

Work embroidery. Exterior fabric (right side) Center (attach ribbon here)

2 Trace the finished dimensions for the
lining fabric on the reverse side of each
piece, as shown, and cut the fabric, adding
a ½" seam allowance on all four sides.

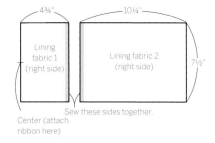

Lining fabric 1 (right side) — 4¾"
Lining fabric 2 (right side) — 10¼" — 7½"
Sew these sides together.
Center (attach ribbon here)

3 Assemble the lining fabric from step 2
with right sides together, and sew one
side. Press the seam allowances open.

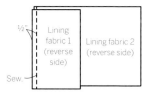

½" Lining fabric 1 (reverse side) Lining fabric 2 (reverse side) Sew.

4 Assemble the exterior fabric from step 1
and the lining fabric from step 3 with right
sides together. Insert the ribbon between
the fabrics at the center, as shown. Sew
around all four sides, leaving an opening
for turning out.

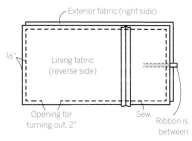

Exterior fabric (right side)
½" Lining fabric (reverse side)
Opening for turning out, 2" Sew. Ribbon is between

5 Turn right side out, and lightly iron to
reshape. With a U-shaped ladder stitch,
sew the opening closed.

6 Fold the side opposite where the ribbon
is attached 5¼" toward the interior. Use a
slipstitch to sew both sides.
*You can also machine stitch.

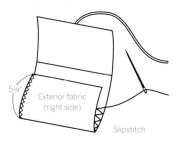

5¼" Exterior fabric (right side) Slipstitch

MAKE YOUR OWN TASSEL
MATERIALS
No. 25 embroidery floss, 1 skein
Thicker thread, 6"

HOW TO MAKE

1 Cut 11¾" piece of embroidery floss and
thread it through a needle. Make a loop with
the thicker thread and tie a square knot.

2 Hold the middle of the skein of embroidery
floss and the doubled thread on the
needle from step 1. Wrap the thread on
the needle around the skein, as if to fasten
it. Pull the wrapped thread tight, and pass
the needle through the middle.

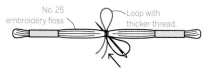

No. 25 embroidery floss Loop with thicker thread.

3 Fold the skein from step 2 in half. Wrap it
again with the thread on the needle, ½"
from the fold, and fasten firmly as in step
2. To finish, cut the skein to the desired
length.

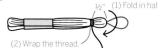

½" (1) Fold in half.
(2) Wrap the thread.

DANGLING MONKEY
Drawstring Backpack

PAGE 13

FINISHED SIZE
13" x 17" (main part of bag)

NO. 25 EMBROIDERY FLOSS
DMC 645, 648, 842, 310, 733, 505, 1 skein
each

MATERIALS
Exterior fabric: Linen, light gray,
15¾" x 39½"
Lining fabric: Linen, white, 15¾" x 39½"
Loop fabric: Linen, light gray, 3¼" x 3¼",
2 pieces
¼"-wide rayon cord, beige, 5', 2 pieces
*The length of the cord is sized for
children.
Machine-sewing thread, light gray, as
needed

TOOLS
Bodkin

HOW TO MAKE

1 Using an iron, press folds into the fabric for
the loops as shown, and machine stitch
both edges. Fold in half again. Make two.

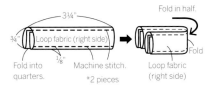

2 Transfer the embroidery pattern (p. 62),
evenly spaced, onto the right side of the
front exterior of the bag. Embroider the
pattern, and iron your work lightly. Trace
the finished dimensions onto the reverse
side, as shown, and cut the fabric,
adding a ½" seam allowance on all four
sides. Cut the lining fabric to the same
dimensions.

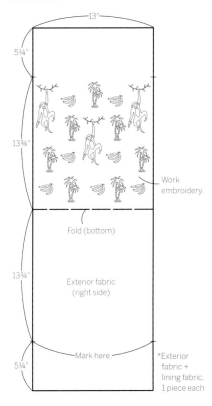

3 Fold the exterior fabric from step 2 in half
with right sides together. Insert the loop
fabric from step 1 between the exterior
and lining at the bottom of both sides.
Sew up to the mark.

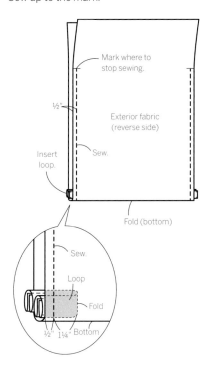

4 Press the seam allowances on both sides
of the exterior bag from step 3 open,
and turn the bag right side out. Make the
interior bag the same way.

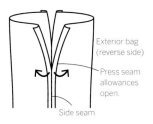

5 Assemble the exterior bag and interior bag with right sides facing out, and sew the sides, as shown.

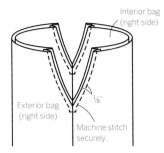

Interior bag
(right side)

Exterior bag
(right side)

⅛"

Machine stitch securely.

6 Make a ½" inward fold along the edge of the mouth of the bag and press. Then make another 2⅜" fold, and machine stitch two rows to create the casing for the cord to pass through. Sew the other side the same way.

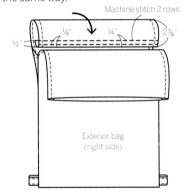

Machine stitch 2 rows.

⅛" ¼" 2⅜"
½"

Exterior bag
(right side)

7 Insert the cords through both sides of the casings from step 6 and then through the loops on the bottom. Tie the ends.

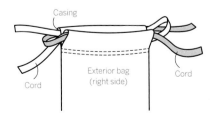

Casing

Cord

Exterior bag
(right side)

Cord

DANCING RABBITS
Trivet Cushion

PAGE 15

FINISHED SIZE
7½" x 7½"

NO. 25 EMBROIDERY FLOSS
DMC 3031, 2 skeins

DMC ecru, 739, 3051, 3777, 823, 830, 310,
    1 skein each

MATERIALS
Exterior fabric: Linen, beige, 17¾" x 9¾"
Machine-sewing thread, beige, as needed
Craft batting, as needed

HOW TO MAKE

1 Transfer the embroidery pattern (p. 63) onto the right side of the exterior fabric, as shown. Embroider the pattern, and iron your work lightly. Trace the finished dimensions onto the reverse side, as shown, and cut the fabric, adding a ½" seam allowance on all four sides.

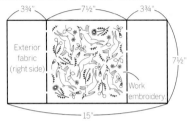

3¾" 7½" 3¾"

Exterior
fabric
(right side)

7½"

Work
embroidery

15"

2 Fold the fabric in half lengthwise, right sides together, and sew along the edge, leaving an opening for turning out. Press the seam allowances open.

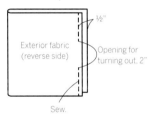

Exterior fabric
(reverse side)

½"

Opening for
turning out, 2"

Sew.

3 Make a crease on each side to center the seam from step 2. Sew the top and bottom edges together.

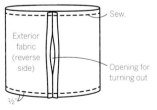

Sew.

Exterior
fabric
(reverse
side)

Opening for
turning out

½"

4 Turn right side out, and lightly iron to reshape. Stuff as much craft batting inside as needed. Sew the opening closed with a U-shaped ladder stitch.

WILD REINDEER
Simple Bag

PAGE 17

FINISHED SIZE
8¼" x 11½"

NO. 25 EMBROIDERY FLOSS
DMC ecru, 926, 2 skeins each
DMC 08, 310, 1 skein each

MATERIALS
Exterior fabric: Linen, black, 9¾" x 25½"
Lining fabric: Linen, white, 9¾" x 25½"
Shoulder strap fabric: Linen, black,
   43¼" x 1½"
Machine-sewing thread, black, as needed

HOW TO MAKE

1 Using an iron, press folds into the fabric for the shoulder strap, as shown. Machine stitch both edges.

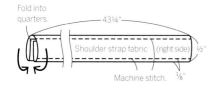

Fold into quarters.

43¼"

Shoulder strap fabric | (right side) | ½"

Machine stitch. | ⅛"

2 Transfer the embroidery pattern (p. 64), evenly spaced, onto the right side of the front exterior of the bag. Embroider the pattern, and iron your work lightly. Trace the finished dimensions onto the reverse side, as shown, and cut the fabric, adding a ½" seam allowance on all four sides. Cut the lining fabric to the same dimensions.

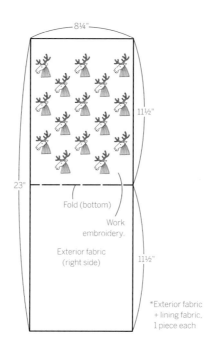

8¼"

11½"

23"

Fold (bottom)

Work embroidery.

Exterior fabric (right side)

11½"

*Exterior fabric + lining fabric, 1 piece each

3 Fold the exterior fabric from step 2 in half, right sides together, and sew the left and right sides. Press the seam allowances open. Sew the lining fabric in the same way, leaving an opening for turning out.

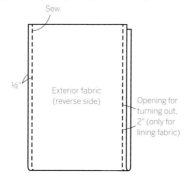

Sew.

½"

Exterior fabric (reverse side)

Opening for turning out, 2" (only for lining fabric)

4 Assemble the exterior bag and interior bag, right sides together. Then insert the shoulder strap fabric from step 1 at both sides, between the exterior and interior bags. Sew all the way around the mouth of the bag.

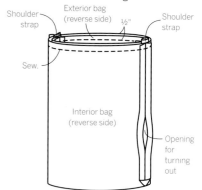

Shoulder strap

Exterior bag (reverse side)

½"

Shoulder strap

Sew.

Interior bag (reverse side)

Opening for turning out

5 Turn right side out, and lightly iron to reshape. With a U-shaped ladder stitch, sew the opening closed.

WOOLLY SHEEP
Needle Case

PAGE 19

FINISHED SIZE
4" x 3¼"

NO. 25 EMBROIDERY FLOSS
DMC 310, 712, 3790, 1 skein each

MATERIALS
Exterior fabric: Linen, beige, 9¾" x 6"
Lining fabric: Linen, beige, 9¾" x 6"
Felt, brown, 6¾" x 2½"
Single-sided fusible quilt batting, 8" x 3¼"
¾"-diameter wooden button, 1 piece
⅛"-wide cord, brown, 2¼" long
Machine-sewing thread, beige, as needed

HOW TO MAKE

1. Transfer the embroidery pattern (p. 64) onto the right side of the exterior fabric, as shown. Embroider the pattern, and iron your work lightly. Trace the finished dimensions onto the reverse side, and cut the fabric, adding a ½" seam allowance on all four sides. Cut the lining fabric to the same dimensions.

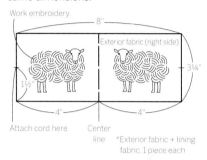

Work embroidery.

8"

Exterior fabric (right side)

3¼"

1½"

4"   4"

Attach cord here.   Center line   *Exterior fabric + lining fabric, 1 piece each

2. Assemble the exterior fabric and the lining fabric, right sides together, with the cord folded in half and inserted at the center mark. Sew around all four sides, leaving an opening for turning out. Place the fusible side of the quilt batting on the reverse side of the embroidered work, and if you're using a pressing cloth, lay that on top before using an iron to activate the adhesive. *Before applying the fusible quilt, make sure that any wrinkles in the exterior fabric have been smoothed out.

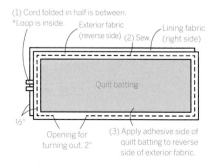

(1) Cord folded in half is between.
*Loop is inside.   Exterior fabric (reverse side)   (2) Sew.   Lining fabric (right side)

Quilt batting

½"

Opening for turning out, 2"   (3) Apply adhesive side of quilt batting to reverse side of exterior fabric.

3. When the fabric from step 2 is cool and the quilt batting has fully adhered, turn right side out and lightly iron to reshape. With a U-shaped ladder stitch, sew the opening closed.

4. Place the felt on the interior (the side that is not embroidered), aligning it along the center line, and machine stitch the center line.

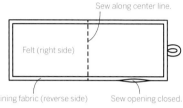

Sew along center line.

Felt (right side)

Lining fabric (reverse side)   Sew opening closed.

5. Attach the button to the exterior fabric.

Exterior fabric (right side)   Button

GIRAFFES ON THE SAVANNA
Sachet

PAGE 21

FINISHED SIZE
4¾" x 4¾"

NO. 25 EMBROIDERY FLOSS
DMC 712, 829, 938, 520, 522, 310, 1 skein each

MATERIALS
Exterior fabric: Linen, white, 8" x 8", 2 pieces
String for hanging: DMC No. 5 embroidery floss, blanc, 11¾"

Craft batting, as needed
Your choice of herbs, as needed
*Wrap herbs in gauze.
Machine-sewing thread, white, as needed

HOW TO MAKE

1. Transfer the embroidery pattern (p. 65) onto the right side of the center of one piece of exterior fabric, as shown. Embroider the pattern, and iron your work lightly. Assemble both pieces of exterior fabric, right sides together, and sew around the pattern, about ½" away, leaving an opening for turning out.

2. Cut away the excess fabric, adding a ¼" seam allowance outside the sewn stitches. Make cuts along the seam allowances of the curves, and turn the project right side out. Insert craft batting and your choice of herbs, and then sew the opening closed with a U-shaped ladder stitch. Sew the string in place for hanging.

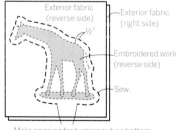

Exterior fabric (reverse side)   Exterior fabric (right side)

½"

Embroidered work (reverse side)

Sew.

Make opening for turning out on bottom.

CHEETAH IN THE JUNGLE
Mini Tote Bag

PAGE 23

FINISHED SIZE
7" x 7" (main part of bag)

NO. 25 EMBROIDERY FLOSS
DMC 3371, 833, 3046, 869, 890, 520,
    3687, 543, 1 skein each

MATERIALS
Exterior fabric: Linen, pale pink, 9¾" x 15¾"
Lining fabric: Linen, white, 9¾" x 15¾"
Handle fabric: Linen, pale pink,
    11¾" x 1½", 2 pieces
Machine-sewing thread, pale pink, as
    needed

HOW TO MAKE

1 Using an iron, press folds into the fabric
   for the handles, as shown, and machine
   stitch both edges. Make two.

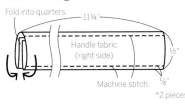

Fold into quarters.
11¾"
Handle fabric
(right side)
½"
Machine stitch.
⅛"
*2 pieces

2 Transfer the embroidery pattern (p. 66)
   onto the right side of the front exterior
   of the bag. Embroider the pattern, and
   iron your work lightly. Trace the finished
   dimensions onto the reverse side, as
   shown, and cut the fabric, adding a ½"
   seam allowance on all four sides. Cut the
   lining fabric to the same dimensions.

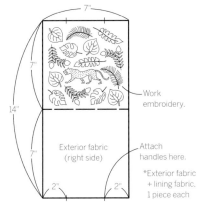

7"
7"
14"
7"
2"
2"
Work
embroidery.
Exterior fabric
(right side)
Attach
handles here.
*Exterior fabric
+ lining fabric,
1 piece each

3 Fold the exterior fabric from step 2 in half,
   right sides together, and sew both sides
   together, leaving an opening for turning
   out. Press the seam allowances open. Sew
   the lining fabric in the same way, leaving
   an opening for turning out.
   *The process is the same as step 3 on p. 84.

4 Assemble the exterior bag and interior bag,
   right sides together. Insert the fabric for the
   handles from step 1 on each side, between
   the exterior and interior bags, and sew all
   the way around the mouth of the bag.
   *You can reinforce where the handles are
   attached by backstitching several times.

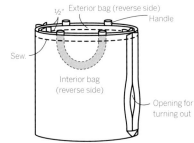

½"
Exterior bag (reverse side)
Handle
Sew.
Interior bag
(reverse side)
Opening for
turning out

5 Turn right side out, and lightly iron to
   reshape. With a U-shaped ladder stitch,
   sew the opening closed.

CAT FACES
Note Card

PAGE 25

FINISHED SIZE
3¼" x 3¼"

NO. 25 EMBROIDERY FLOSS
*For gray cat
DMC 310, 733, 648, 645, 1 skein each

MATERIALS
Exterior fabric: Linen, light gray, 6" x 6"
Outer card: Heavy paper stock, light gray,
    3¼" x 6¾"
Inner card: Heavy paper stock, light gray, 3" x 3"
Double-sided tape (thin type), as needed

HOW TO MAKE
Transfer the embroidery pattern (p. 67) onto
the right side of the exterior fabric. Embroider
the pattern, and iron your work lightly. Trace
and cut the pattern for the outer card (p. 95),
fold it in half, and then cut out the cat shape
with a utility knife. Assemble the project so the
embroidered work shows through the cut-out,
and trim the excess exterior fabric so that it's
slightly smaller than the inner card. Using the
double-sided tape, attach the fabric with the
embroidery between the inner and outer cards.

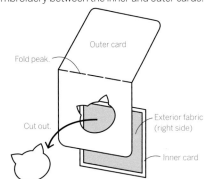

Outer card
Fold peak.
Cut out.
Exterior fabric
(right side)
Inner card

DOGS AND BONES
Tote Bag

PAGE 27

FINISHED SIZE
11¾" x 8" (main part of bag) x 3¼"
(gusset)

NO. 25 EMBROIDERY FLOSS
DMC 3865, 2 skeins
DMC 3799, 801, 829, 07, 08, 1 skein each

MATERIALS
Exterior fabric: Linen, sand, 13¾" x 21¾"
Lining fabric: Linen, white, 13¾" x 17¾"
Facing fabric: Linen, sand, 13¾" x 6"
Handle fabric: Linen, sand, 13¾" x 4",
    2 pieces
Machine-sewing thread, sand, as needed

HOW TO MAKE

1 Using an iron, press folds into the fabric
for the handles, as shown, and machine
stitch both edges. Make two.

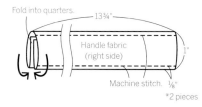

2 Transfer the embroidery pattern (p. 68)
onto the right side of the exterior of the
bag. Embroider the pattern, and iron your
work lightly. Trace the project dimensions
(p. 93) onto the reverse side, as shown, and
cut the fabric, adding a ½" seam allowance
on all four sides.

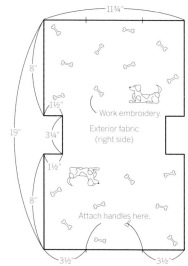

3 For the facing fabric and the lining fabric,
trace the finished dimensions as shown
below on the reverse sides of each piece,
and cut, adding a ½" seam allowance on
all four sides. Cut two pieces of facing
fabric.

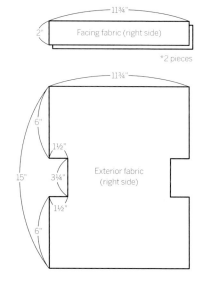

4 Assemble the facing fabric at the top and
bottom of the opening of the bag, right sides
together, and sew. Fold the exterior fabric in
half, right sides together, and sew both sides.
Spread open the lining fabric and the facing
fabric, then sew both sides in the same way,
leaving an opening for turning out.

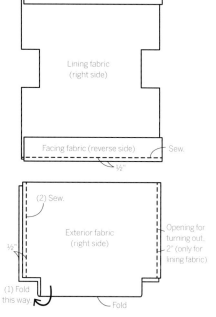

5 Press the seam allowances on both sides
of the exterior bag open, then flatten the
side seams in order to sew the edges of the
bottom together. Repeat with the interior bag.

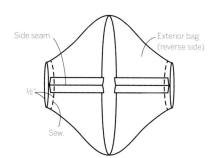

6 Assemble the exterior bag and interior bag from step 5 with right sides together. Insert the fabric for the handles on each side, between the exterior and interior bags, and sew all the way around the mouth of the bag. Turn right side out, and lightly iron to reshape. With a U-shaped ladder stitch, sew the opening closed.

KNIGHT
Brooch

PAGE 29

FINISHED SIZE
1¼" x 2¼"

NO. 25 EMBROIDERY FLOSS
*For brown version
DMC 3031, 829, 310, 1 skein each
*For white version
DMC 02, 03, 310, 1 skein each

MATERIALS
Exterior fabric: Linen, black, 6" x 6", 2 pieces
Brooch pin, gold, 1 piece
Craft batting, as needed
Machine-sewing thread, black, as needed

HOW TO MAKE

1 Transfer the embroidery pattern (p. 68) onto the right side of the center of one piece of exterior fabric, as shown. Embroider the pattern, then iron your work lightly. Assemble with the other piece of exterior fabric, right sides together, and sew around the pattern, about ¼" away, leaving an opening for turning out.

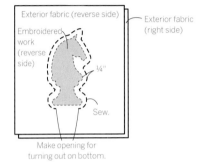

2 Cut away the excess fabric, adding a ¼" seam allowance outside the sewn stitches. Make cuts along the seam allowances of the curves, and turn right side out.

3 Insert craft batting, and sew the opening closed with a U-shaped ladder stitch. Attach the brooch pin to the back.

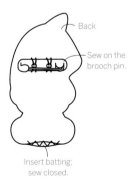

WOLVES AT NIGHT
Drawstring Bag

PAGE 31

FINISHED SIZE
9¾" x 9¾" (main part of bag)

NO. 25 EMBROIDERY FLOSS
DMC 319, 2 skeins
DMC 3768, 733, 3790, 1 skein each

MATERIALS
Exterior fabric: Linen, light blue, 21¾" x 11¾"
Lining fabric: Linen, white, 21¾" x 11¾"
Casing fabric: Linen, light blue, 9¾" x 6"
Shoulder strap fabric: Linen, light blue, 43¼" x 1½"
⅛"-wide round cord, light blue, 31½", 2 pieces
Machine-sewing thread, light blue, as needed

TOOLS
Bodkin

HOW TO MAKE

1 Using an iron, press folds into the fabric for the shoulder strap, as shown, and machine stitch both edges.

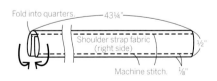

2 Cut the fabric for the casings, adding a ½" seam allowance on all four sides. On the short ends, fold the seam allowances. Machine stitch, and fold the piece in half again lengthwise.

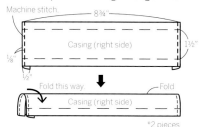

3 Transfer the embroidery pattern (p. 69) onto the right side of the front exterior of the bag, as shown. Embroider the pattern, and iron your work lightly. Trace the project dimensions (p. 94) onto the reverse side (as shown), and cut the fabric, adding a ½" seam allowance on all four sides. Cut another exterior piece of fabric. Cut two pieces of lining fabric to the same dimensions.

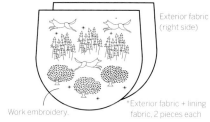

4 Assemble the exterior fabric from step 3, right sides together, and sew around the edge, leaving the mouth open. Sew the lining fabric in the same way, leaving an opening for turning out. Make cuts along the seam allowances of the curves.

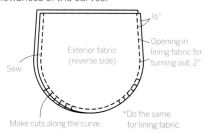

5 Assemble the exterior bag and interior bag from step 4, right sides together. Insert the casings from step 2 on both sides with the folds facing downward and the shoulder strap from step 1 at the side seams—all between the exterior and interior bags, as shown. Sew around the mouth of the bag.

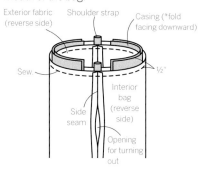

6 Turn right side out, and lightly iron to reshape. With a U-shaped ladder stitch, sew the opening closed.

7 Insert the round cords through both sides of the casings, and tie the ends.

OWLS AND MOONS
Charm Pouch

PAGE 33

FINISHED SIZE
2¾" x 4¼"

NO. 25 EMBROIDERY FLOSS
DMC 3865, 834, 07, 08, 3371, 310, 1 skein each

MATERIALS
Exterior fabric: Linen, white, 6" x 6", 2 pieces
¼-inch-wide ribbon, gold lamé, 6", 2 pieces
Machine-sewing thread, white, as needed

HOW TO MAKE
1 Transfer the embroidery pattern (p. 69) onto the right side of the exterior fabric. Embroider the pattern, and iron it lightly. Trace the project dimensions (p. 95) onto the reverse side, and cut the fabric, adding a ½" seam allowance on all four sides. Cut another exterior piece of fabric.

2 Make a double inward fold on the mouth of the exterior fabric, as shown, and machine stitch it in place. Do the same for the other piece of exterior fabric.

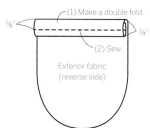

3 Assemble the two pieces of exterior fabric, right sides together, and insert the two pieces of ribbon between the pieces of fabric at the attachment mark. Sew around the edge, leaving the mouth open. Trim the excess fabric from the seam allowance, leaving a ¼" seam allowance, and make cuts along the curves.

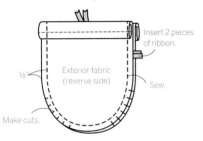

Insert 2 pieces of ribbon.
½"
Exterior fabric (reverse side)
Sew.
Make cuts.

4 Turn right side out, press to reshape, and machine stitch about ⅛" from the edge all around.
*You can also sew this by hand.

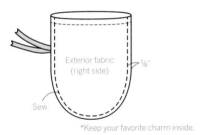

Exterior fabric (right side)
⅛"
Sew.
*Keep your favorite charm inside.

CIRCUS ELEPHANTS
Triangular Flags

PAGE 35

FINISHED SIZE
4¾" wide x 4¾" high

NO. 25 EMBROIDERY FLOSS
DMC 22, 712, 646, 310, 1 skein each

MATERIALS
Exterior fabric: Linen, white, 6" x 11¾", 2 pieces
½"-sized bell, silver, 1 piece
String: DMC No. 5 embroidery floss, blanc, 15¾", 2 pieces
Hand-sewing thread, color that matches fabric, as needed
Machine-sewing thread, white, as needed

HOW TO MAKE
1 Transfer the embroidery pattern (p. 95) onto the right side of the exterior fabric. Embroider the pattern, and iron your work lightly. Trace the project dimensions (p. 95) onto the reverse side, and cut out, adding a ½" seam allowance on all four sides.

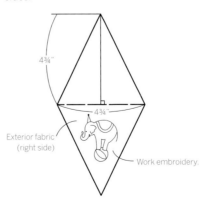

4¾"
4¾"
Exterior fabric (right side)
Work embroidery.

2 Fold the exterior fabric in half, right sides together, and sew the two sides, leaving an opening for turning out. Turn right side out, and lightly iron to reshape. With a U-shaped ladder stitch, sew the opening closed.

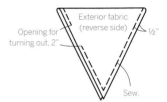

Opening for turning out, 2"
Exterior fabric (reverse side)
½"
Sew.

3 Attach the bell to the bottom point with hand-sewing thread. Make as many more of the same flags as you like, string them together with hand-sewing thread, and hang them from string tied to each end.

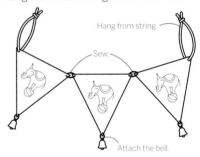

Hang from string.
Sew.
Attach the bell.

DEER EMBLEM
Scissors Case

PAGE 37

FINISHED SIZE
4" x 5¼"

NO. 25 EMBROIDERY FLOSS
DMC ecru, 829, 500, 3031, 407, 1 skein each

MATERIALS

Exterior fabric: Linen, dark gray, 6" x 9¾"
Lining fabric: Linen, dark gray, 6" x 9¾"
Single-sided fusible quilt batting, 6" x 9¾"
Protective fabric: Felt, black, 2" x 4"
⅛"-wide double-sided velveteen ribbon,
　　black, 8", 2 pieces
Machine-sewing thread, dark gray, as needed
Wood glue

HOW TO MAKE

1 Transfer the embroidery pattern (p. 70)
onto the right side of the exterior fabric.
Embroider the pattern, and iron your work
lightly. Trace the project dimensions (p. 70)
onto the reverse side, and cut the fabric,
adding a ½" seam allowance all around. Cut
out another exterior piece of fabric, and cut
out two pieces of lining fabric to the same
dimensions.

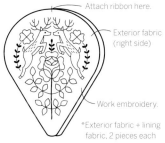

Attach ribbon here.

Exterior fabric
(right side)

Work embroidery.

*Exterior fabric + lining
fabric, 2 pieces each

2 Assemble the exterior fabric and lining
fabric, right sides together, and insert one
piece of ribbon at the center. Sew around the
outside edge, leaving an opening for turning
out. Make cuts along the curves of the seam
allowance. Assemble the other set in the
same way. Cut the single-sided fusible quilt
batting to fit the pattern, place the fusible
side on the reverse side of the embroidered
piece, and, if you're using a pressing cloth,
lay that on top before using an iron to
activate the adhesive. Apply the quilt batting
to the other piece in the same way.

*Before applying the fusible quilt batting,
make sure that any wrinkles in the exterior
fabric have been smoothed out.

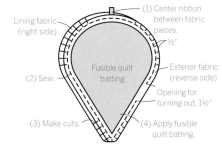

Lining fabric
(right side)

(1) Center ribbon
between fabric
pieces.
½"

Exterior fabric
(reverse side)

(2) Sew.

Fusible quilt
batting

Opening for
turning out. 1½"

(3) Make cuts.

(4) Apply fusible
quilt batting.

3 Allow the fabric from step 2 to cool and
the quilt batting to fully adhere. Turn right
side out, and lightly iron to reshape. With
a U-shaped ladder stitch, sew the opening
closed. Cut the felt so it's slightly smaller
than the point of the lining side and attach it
with wood glue.
*The felt protects the scissors. They will be
even more protected if you use leather.

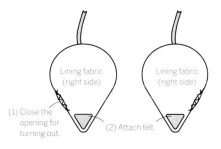

Lining fabric
(right side)

Lining fabric
(right side)

(1) Close the
opening for
turning out.

(2) Attach felt.

4 Allow the glue to dry. Assemble the pieces
with linings together, and whipstitch from one
mark around to the other, creating a pouch.
*You can also machine stitch.

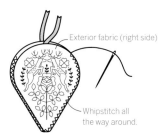

Exterior fabric (right side)

Whipstitch all
the way around.

TEDDY BEARS AND PANDA
Bookmark

PAGE 39

FINISHED SIZE
2¾" x 3¼"

NO. 25 EMBROIDERY FLOSS
DMC 3866, 613, 08, 310, 1 skein each

MATERIALS
Exterior fabric: Linen, white, 6" x 6", 2 pieces
⅛"-wide satin ribbon, red, 6"
Hand-sewing thread, white, as needed

HOW TO MAKE
Transfer the embroidery pattern (p. 71),
centered, onto the right side of one piece
of exterior fabric, as shown. Embroider
the pattern, and iron your work lightly.
Assemble with the other piece of exterior
fabric, right sides together, fold the ribbon
in half, and insert it between the fabric
pieces. Using white embroidery floss, sew
all around the pattern with running stitches,
about ¼" away. Cut out, leaving about ½"
outside of the pattern.
*Finish using whatever shape you prefer.

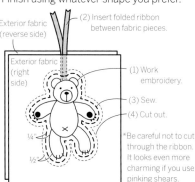

Exterior fabric
(reverse side)

(2) Insert folded ribbon
between fabric pieces.

Exterior fabric
(right
side)

(1) Work
embroidery.

(3) Sew.

(4) Cut out.

¼"

½"

*Be careful not to cut
through the ribbon.
It looks even more
charming if you use
pinking shears.

Project Patterns

BEARS IN THE FOREST
Crossbody Bag

PAGE 80

Enlarge by 220%
Embroidery pattern on page 58

Exterior fabric, 2 pieces

DOGS AND BONES
Tote Bag

Enlarge by 160%
Embroidery pattern on page 68

PAGE 87

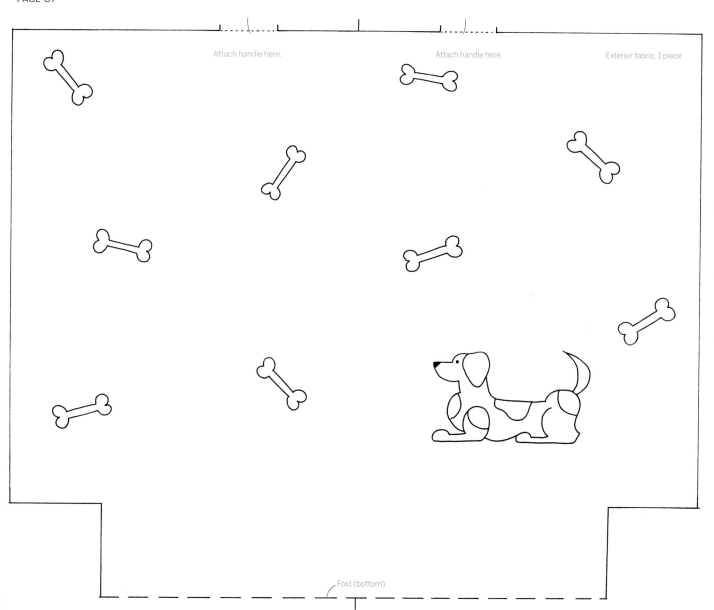

Attach handle here.

Attach handle here.

Exterior fabric. 1 piece

Fold (bottom)

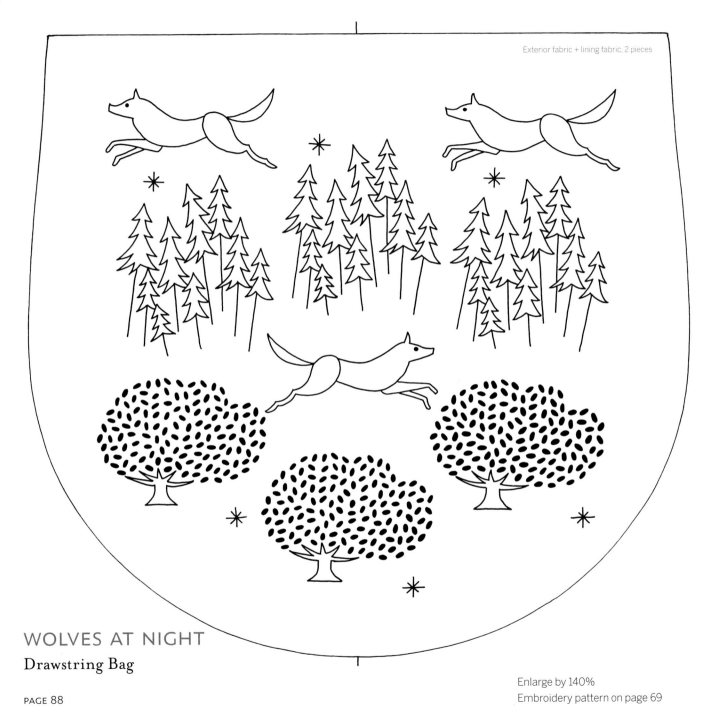

Exterior fabric + lining fabric, 2 pieces

WOLVES AT NIGHT
Drawstring Bag

PAGE 88

Enlarge by 140%
Embroidery pattern on page 69

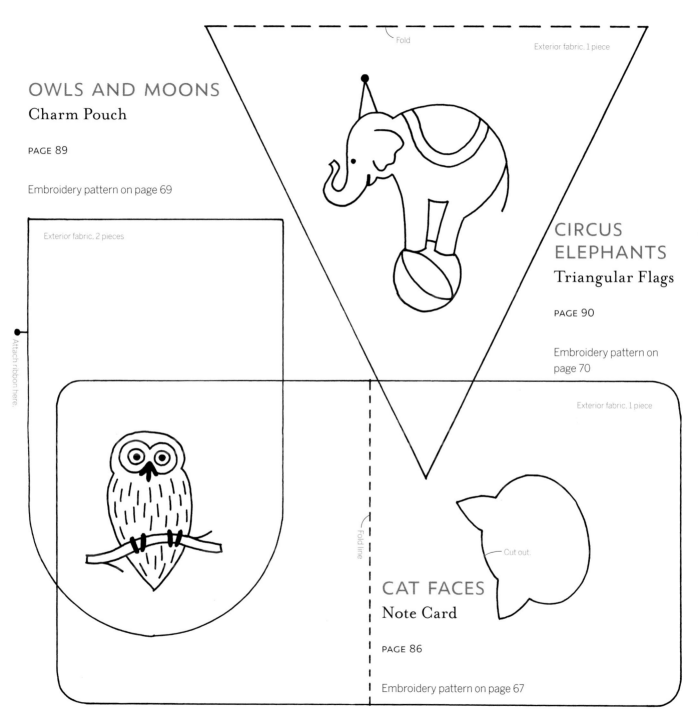

OWLS AND MOONS
Charm Pouch

PAGE 89

Embroidery pattern on page 69

Exterior fabric, 2 pieces

Attach ribbon here.

Fold

Exterior fabric, 1 piece

CIRCUS
ELEPHANTS
Triangular Flags

PAGE 90

Embroidery pattern on page 70

Exterior fabric, 1 piece

Fold line

Cut out.

CAT FACES
Note Card

PAGE 86

Embroidery pattern on page 67

YUMIKO HIGUCHI

After graduating from Tama Art University, Yumiko Higuchi worked as a handbag designer. Her pieces were shown and sold in boutiques. She began creating embroidery designs in 2008. She produces original embroidery patterns that feature botanical motifs and all manner of insects and living creatures.

ROOST BOOKS
An imprint of Shambhala Publications, Inc.
2129 13th Street
Boulder, Colorado 80302
www.roostbooks.com

Translation © 2021 by Shambhala Publications, Inc.
Translation by Allison Markin Powell
Originally published as *Higuchi Yumiko no dobutsu shishu*
© 2019 by Yumiko Higuchi
Educational Foundation Bunka Gakuen Bunka Publishing Bureau

English translation rights arranged with Educational Foundation Bunka Gakuen, Bunka Publishing Bureau through Japan UNI Agency, Inc., Tokyo

BUNKA PUBLISHING BUREAU STAFF CREDITS
Book Design: Kana Tsukada (ME & MIRACO)
Photography: Aya Sunahara (p. 2–51), Kaori Murao
Styling: Kaori Maeda
Hair and Makeup: Yuki Oike
Model: Alek Helms (Sugar & Spice)
DTP: WADE Handicraft Production Department
Proofreader: Masako Mukai
Editors: Mariko Tsuchiya (Three Season); Kaoru Tanaka (Bunka Publishing Bureau)
Publisher: Katsuhiro Hamada

9 8 7 6 5 4 3 2

Printed in China

♻This edition is printed on acid-free paper that meets the American National Standards Institute Z39.48 Standard.
♻Shambhala Publications makes every effort to print on recycled paper. For more information please visit www.shambhala.com. Roost Books is distributed worldwide by Penguin Random House, Inc., and its subsidiaries.

ISBN: 978-1-61180-886-5

Library of Congress Control Number: 2020947443